CAST OF

GOKU

He looks like a normal guy, but he's actually something much more.

BULMA

This tough speedster-riding girl is also after the legendary Dragon Balls!

CHI CHI

The girl at school Goku has a crush on has secrets of her own!

CHARACTERS

MASTER ROSHI

His secrets
may help Goku
save the world!

LORD PICCOLO

If he finds the
Dragon Balls
before Goku,
all is lost!

DRAGONBALL
EVOLUTION

THE DISCOVERY

by Stacia Deutsch & Rhody Cohon

Screenplay by Ben Ramsey
Based upon the graphic novel series "Dragonball" by Akira Toriyama

vizkids
VIZ MEDIA
SAN FRANCISCO

DRAGONBALL: EVOLUTION
The Discovery

Adapted by Stacia Deutsch & Rhody Cohon
Based on the motion picture screenplay by Ben Ramsey

Design: Carolina Ugalde

Published by VIZ Media, LLC
P.O. Box 77010
San Francisco, CA 94107

www.viz.com
www.vizkids.com

Library of Congress Cataloging-in-Publication Data

Deutsch, Stacia.
  Dragonball evolution. Chapter book 1. The discovery / adapted by Stacia Deutsch and Rhody Cohon.
    p. cm. -- (Dragon ball)
  "From the screenplay by Ben Ramsey"--Copr. p.
  ISBN 1-4215-2661-1
  I. Cohon, Rhody. II. Ramsey, Ben. III. Dragonball evolution (Motion picture) IV. Title. V. Title: Discovery.
  PZ7.D4953Dr 2009
  [Fic]--dc22
                    2008020234

Printed in the U.S.A.
First printing, February 2009

CHAPTER ONE

"THE FIRST ONE to touch the ground loses," Gohan told his grandson. The old man might have been seventy years old, but he could still move like a kung fu expert.

Goku stared deeply into his grandfather's eyes. He was ready to fight, even if it was just for practice.

Goku was standing on two wires, usually used to hang laundry. The wires were high and strung tightly between two wooden poles. He was balancing with one foot on each wire.

Gohan stood on one of the wooden poles.

He spun his bow staff across his body. The rod moved so fast the staff was almost invisible. Then he struck. Goku ducked, dodging his grandfather's blows.

Goku used the wires under his feet like a spring. He bounced up, then got busy with a fast bunch of kicks and punches. The old man had to weave back and forth to avoid Goku's blows.

"Prepare to eat dirt," Gohan warned. He swung his bow staff in a mighty arc.

Leaping, dodging, and flipping, Goku stayed on the wire, but he knew he needed to take the lead in this battle. And soon.

There! Goku's eyes caught sight of a little bug crawling on the laundry line.

With a solid flip, Goku landed near the bug. He stomped on the wire, and the bug flew into the air. Goku smacked at the little bug with his hand and sent it right into Gohan's mouth!

Gohan choked, caught by surprise as he swallowed the small bug. In that second, Goku found the chance he needed to win the fight.

Goku caught the bow staff in his hands and tore it out of Gohan's grasp. He threw the staff into the garden below.

Certain that he'd won the game, Goku slowed for a second. One last kick and the old man would fall to the garden too. Goku leapt into a powerful flying side-kick.

But Gohan was a master fighter. The old

man brought his hand to his chest, then pushed out a blast of energy. Power waves from the old man's *Ki*, his energy force, struck the flying boy.

Goku fell out of the sky onto the soft earth. His head crashed against a melon in the garden.

Gohan leapt down from the laundry line. He came over to help Goku up.

"Shadow Crane Strike," Gohan explained. He reached over to dust dirt off of Goku. "You fell for it again."

Goku wiped melon seeds from the side of his face. "It's not easy to block a move that I can't see."

"True power comes from inside." Gohan placed one wrinkled hand against Goku's chest. "Your Ki is your best defense and your greatest weapon." He tapped the spot over Goku's heart. "Feel the energy here."

Goku felt that fighting with Ki was just too hard. He'd rather use his muscles.

"Focus the power," Gohan told him.

Goku tried to use his Ki. He lifted his hand, palm facing outward. Then he pushed forward, like Gohan had. Nothing happened.

Goku looked at his grandfather. "See?"

"To use your Ki," Gohan instructed, "you must be at one not only with yourself, but also your enemy." Gohan pointed to a tree in the garden. "Pretend that tree is your enemy."

Goku sighed and closed his eyes. He tried hard to channel his energy. A breeze swept through the tree leaves, but it was just the wind blowing. Not Goku's Ki.

"Sorry, Grandpa. I didn't feel a thing." Goku opened his eyes.

"Someday, Goku," Gohan said with a small nod.

Goku laughed. "Yeah," he said. "Someday I'll beat you."

Gohan grinned wildly. "Yes. You can tell all your friends how you beat up a seventy-year-old man."

Goku stopped laughing and gave a sad smile. "What friends?" The mood turned sour. "Everyone at school treats me like I'm nothing, Grandpa. I don't fit into any group."

Gohan placed an arm around his grand-son. "You're special, Goku."

"No." Goku stepped away. "I'm strange. I know it. The other kids know it too." He kicked a rock. "Sometimes they are so mean to me, I want to explode."

Gohan shook his head slowly. "I don't train you to fight with boys at school."

Goku felt mad. "Why am I doing this? If I can't fight, then teach me something I can use. Like how to fit in." Goku turned away from his grandfather. He didn't think the old man knew how hard it really was for him.

Gohan tried to cheer the boy up. He reached into his pocket. "Happy eighteenth birthday," he said, holding out a small gift to his grandson.

Goku relaxed, then smiled. He took the package and tore off the brown paper.

Inside was a small ball. The surface was smooth like a pearl. Four stars floated inside the ball. Goku rolled it around in his hand.

"Sushinchu is yours," Gohan told him.

"What is it?" Goku asked.

"It's a Dragon Ball," Gohan explained. "*Sushinchu* means 'four stars.' In the entire world there are only six other Dragon Balls. From one to seven stars."

"What does it do?" Goku turned the ball over and over.

"By itself, nothing," his grandfather said. "But together, it is said the seven Dragon Balls will grant the holder one perfect wish." Gohan reached over to wrap Goku's hand around the Dragon Ball. "Keep it safe. Always," Gohan said.

"Thanks, Grandpa." Goku slipped the Dragon Ball into his pocket. He didn't believe in wishes and magic. But if the Dragon Ball was important to his grandpa, he'd take care of it.

"You're a man now!" Gohan cheered. "Tonight, we will celebrate. I will cook all your favorites."

CHAPTER TWO

Goku rode a beat-up scooter to school. It barely worked, but it was all he had. Now he needed a parking space for it.

There! Right at the front of the high school lot. The perfect spot.

Goku pulled into the space and started to flip the kickstand down. The roar of another engine caught his attention.

A speedster zoomed around the parking lot. It came to a stop right on top of Goku's scooter, crushing it. Goku barely had time to dive out of the way.

A big, tough football player got out of the car. It was Carey Fuller. Goku didn't like Fuller. He was a bully who acted like he owned the school.

"Hey, Fuller," Goku called out. "You just wrecked my scooter."

Fuller pretended not to hear Goku. He turned to one of his buddies, a big football player named Agundes. "Agundes," he said. "Did you fart? I thought I heard something."

With a snicker, Agundes nodded toward Goku. "No man. You heard a squeak from him."

Goku was so angry. If only his grand-father would let him fight. He knew he could beat these guys.

Fuller pushed Goku, trying to start a fight.

Goku didn't react. He'd promised his grandfather he wouldn't.

He had to suck it up and walk away.

Goku's science teacher, Mr. Kingery, was talking about a solar eclipse.

"A solar eclipse is very rare," he said, "but we are going to have one in two weeks." Mr. Kingery looked around the room and asked, "What causes eclipses?"

Goku sank down in his chair. He hated it when Mr. Kingery called on him.

He only took this class because a girl named Chi Chi took it too. He wasn't really friends with her. He'd never had the courage to talk to her before. She sat two rows away.

Mr. Kingery called on a know-it-all named Weaver.

"A solar eclipse is when the moon blocks the sun," Weaver answered.

"Correct!" Mr. Kingery nodded happily. He looked around the class for another victim.

"Goku," Mr. Kingery said, "What would our ancestors say about the upcoming solar eclipse?"

Goku didn't know the answer. He looked around the classroom. He wanted someone to help him answer. No one would even meet his eyes. He was on his own.

"Uh…" Goku had no clue. "My grandfather would say, 'Beware of the Nameks.'"

Mr. Kingery was puzzled. "Nameks?" he asked.

"They're an alien race that almost destroyed Earth two thousand years ago." The whole class was looking at Goku like he was a freak.

Would he ever fit in?

Between classes, students grabbed what they needed for the next period.

Goku noticed that Chi Chi, the girl from his class, was having trouble. Her locker wouldn't open.

Chi Chi kept swiping her ID card in the card reader. Instead of a green light, the red light kept blinking.

Chi Chi banged on her locker door. It still

wouldn't open.

Moving out of the shadows, Goku took a step forward. He wanted to help, but then he stopped. Whenever Goku saw Chi Chi, he felt shy and didn't know what to do or say.

Back in the shadows, Goku continued to watch her struggle.

Chi Chi was getting mad. She pulled on the locker's handle until she hurt her hand. She shook it in pain.

Goku looked around at the now empty hallway. Maybe he could help without actually talking to her. He focused his energy in his chest just like Gohan had shown him. He raised his hand, palm out.

Goku surprised himself. When he pressed his hand forward, every locker on Chi Chi's side of the hallway popped open. Papers and books fell out of almost every locker.

Goku was shocked that using his Ki had worked! It wasn't perfect, but at least he'd done it.

Chi Chi turned around to see who had just opened all the lockers. She saw Goku standing there. His palm was still raised.

Goku got nervous and started to walk away.

"Stop!" Chi Chi called after him. He froze. "Hey…Goku, right?"

Goku turned to face her. He lifted his eyes to meet hers.

"Did you do that?" Chi Chi asked. She pointed at all the open lockers.

Goku had trouble speaking. "Uh…yeah. It

was something my grandpa taught me."

"You used your Ki." Chi Chi grinned at Goku.

"You know about Ki?" he asked. He didn't feel so nervous anymore.

"I know about a lot of things. Just because my name is Chi Chi doesn't make me a complete idiot," she laughed.

Goku didn't know what else to say. He didn't want to say something dumb. So he turned and headed off toward his next class.

Chi Chi called after him. "Hey, Goku. I'm having a party tonight at my house."

Goku stopped. He couldn't help but smile. "I'll be there."

CHAPTER THREE

Gohan hummed while he made Goku's birthday dinner. Fresh vegetables from their garden were frying in a gigantic wok. He cooked chicken feet and a duck-like bird called squab. He left the head on the squabs, special for Goku.

"Dinner's almost ready," he called up to Goku. "Five minutes!" Gohan continued to putter in the kitchen. He was having fun making his grandson's birthday meal.

Upstairs, Goku put on a brand-new shirt.

He was getting ready for Chi Chi's party. Looking in the mirror, he liked his clothes. The problem was his spiky hair. Yep, like always, it was sticking straight up.

Goku grabbed a bottle of extra firm hair gel. He squeezed out a huge gob of the sticky stuff and put it on his head. Finally, his hair was staying down.

TANG! Goku's hair bounced back up. He looked like he had porcupine spikes.

It was no use. Goku's hair would never be flat.

He grabbed his wallet. Goku took one last peek in the mirror, then was ready to take off.

Just as he was about to leave, the Dragon Ball rolled out of his school pants pocket. Goku wasn't sure if he should leave it or take it with him. Gohan had told him to keep the ball safe. So he snatched it up and put it in his jacket pocket. Then Goku climbed out his bedroom window. He jumped two floors down to the ground outside.

He saw his grandfather through the dining room window. Goku felt guilty about leaving. But he really wanted to go to Chi Chi's party, so he hurried off into the night.

When Goku got to Chi Chi's house, the party was in full swing. The music was loud and there were a lot of kids hanging out.

Goku sighed when he noticed Agundes and four other guys standing outside.

He was going to have to walk past them to go inside. Goku kept walking, head down, toward the party.

Agundes looked up and asked, "What are you doing here, Geeko?" He stepped in front of Goku.

"It's Goku. Just going to the party." Goku tried to go around Agundes. He blocked the way.

"I was invited," Goku told him. "I'm not looking for trouble."

Agundes laughed. "Trouble found you, freak. So turn around, walk away. And no one's ever gonna know you were here."

Goku sighed and looked down at his feet. He might as well go back home.

As he turned to leave, Agundes and his friends made fun of him.

Goku stopped. He decided that this time

he wasn't going to back down. Goku faced the bullies. "I made a promise I wouldn't fight," Goku told them. All he wanted was to walk past them, into the party.

"It won't be much of a fight," Agundes snarled. "You'll lose fast!"

Agundes opened with a left jab. Goku was so fast, it looked like he barely moved. Agundes missed. Agundes tried to kick Goku. Again, barely moving, Goku ducked. Agundes kicked the air.

Agundes's friends tried to help. A muscle-bound dude named Hillenbrand lunged at Goku. Hillenbrand was quickly outsmarted by Goku. Then another guy named Moreno tried to tackle Goku. At the exact same second, a mean kid named Butler was coming at Goku with a flying side-kick.

Goku stepped out of their way just in time. The two bullies missed Goku and hit each other instead. They fell to the ground.

A football player named Palmer stepped up. Palmer put all his energy into one big, hard punch. But Goku was ready.

Goku backed up against a parked car. When Palmer punched at him, Goku moved out of the way. Palmer's fist hit the car's window. The glass cracked. Palmer yelled out in pain. He was holding his hand.

Goku had taken out four bullies without a scratch on himself.

Carey Fuller came out of the courtyard. Chi Chi was right behind him.

Fuller saw all his friends lying on the

ground.

"Hello, Chi Chi," Goku said. "Thanks for inviting me to the party."

Fuller looked at Chi Chi. He couldn't believe that she'd invited Goku.

Pulling away from Chi Chi, Fuller called out to Goku, "Loser."

Fuller looked around for a weapon. He pulled an iron rod from Chi Chi's garden.

"No, Carey, stop!" Chi Chi cried out.

Fuller charged, swinging the rod like a madman.

Goku was standing in front of Fuller's car. He simply turned, and Fuller's rod hit his own car.

"Close one," Goku taunted. He had finally found the courage to face the bullies. His grandfather might be mad that Goku used his training to fight. But it felt really, really good to stand up for himself.

"Try again," he teased.

Fuller yelled and attacked again. This time when Goku ducked, Fuller smashed his car's front windshield.

Fuller tried one last time to get Goku, but Goku moved aside just in time. Fuller bumped his head against the car and fell to the ground.

Goku felt happy. He'd faced the bullies and won.

And Chi Chi was smiling at him!

This was going to be a great birthday. The best one ever.

CHAPTER FOUR

Gohan sat on his bamboo mat in the center of the living room. He waited patiently for Goku to return and explain where he went.

A shadow passed behind the curtains. Someone was sneaking around outside. The old man could feel danger in his bones. His bow staff was just out of reach. There was no time to retrieve it.

Suddenly, the front door burst open. A woman stood in the doorway. She was dressed in gleaming red. There were weapons strapped all over her body. She was pretty, but Gohan could tell she was also very dangerous.

The woman attacked Gohan without warning. She threw special knives called shuriken which sliced through the air.

Gohan moved like lightning. Leaping up from his mat, he picked up the bow staff. It quickly became a blur in his hands. He knocked the knives to the ground, one after the next.

Gohan stood, holding his staff at the ready. "Is that all you've got?" he asked her.

Behind the woman, someone else came into the house. He looked younger than he really was. His skin was an odd color, kind of green. His ears were slightly pointed. And his face looked fearsome. This man's power was obvious.

The younger man stared at Goku's grandfather. "Mai," he said to the woman, "it's not here." Without another word, the powerful figure closed his hand into a fist. The house began to shake. Everything that wasn't bolted down began to rattle and fell to the ground.

An invisible force was taking over. Gohan had no power against it. He dropped to his knees. His entire body was tense. Sweat poured from the old man.

The twosome turned and left.

Gohan's house crumbled to the ground, then exploded.

At Chi Chi's party, Goku and Chi Chi were sitting down, talking.

"You're different," Chi Chi said with a laugh.

"I don't want to be different," Goku said.

Chi Chi said, "I like different. I know it's hard to believe, but we're a lot alike. There are things I do that nobody knows about..."

Inside Goku's jacket pocket, the Dragon Ball began to glow. Goku didn't notice.

Goku was glad that Chi Chi liked people who were different. It made him feel better. Maybe they could be friends. "This is the best birthday I've ever had," Goku told her.

All of a sudden, a bad feeling came over Goku. Goosebumps broke out on his neck.

He looked up at the moon. It looked

different. Strange. Blue and bright. And then, green flames flashed on the moon. The flames shot toward Goku.

Goku shook his head and looked at the moon again. The moon looked normal. He could tell Chi Chi didn't notice anything odd.

He still felt like something was wrong. "My grandpa is in trouble," he told Chi Chi. "I have to go." Goku jumped up and ran all the way home.

When Goku arrived, he saw that the house was destroyed.

"Grandpa!" Goku called out. A low moan came from behind a table. Goku began to furiously dig through the rubble.

When he found Gohan, he was barely

breathing. He was in really bad shape. Goku pulled his grandfather outside. "Grandpa, don't move. I'll be right back." Goku didn't want to leave, but he had to go get help.

"No," Gohan whispered. "Stay with me. Not much time left."

Tears filled Goku's eyes. "I'm sorry, Grandpa. I'm sorry I wasn't here. Who did this to you?"

"Nameks," he said. He was struggling to breathe. "Lord Piccolo has returned." He locked eyes with Goku. "Sushinchu is safe?"

"Yes," Goku reached into his pocket and pulled out the Dragon Ball. He showed it to Gohan. It was glowing.

While Goku held the Dragon Ball something weird happened. He saw a vision in his mind:

A large asteroid. Totally covered in flames. The rock plows into the earth. A flash in the cracked burning rock reveals a monstrous red eye. The eye slowly opens...

Surprised by what he saw, Goku dropped the Dragon Ball into the dirt. The glow faded as the ball settled on the ground.

"Find Master Roshi," Gohan instructed. He was barely breathing now. "...In Paozu... tell him... Piccolo has returned... He will know what to do..."

His grandpa had more to say. Goku leaned in to listen.

"Seven Dragon Balls...Must be found...For all men's fate...Will be bound...To battle... Forces of death and fear...And compel... Shen Long to appear..." Gohan could hardly speak.

Goku took his grandfather's hand. "Grandfather, stop. You have to rest."

Gohan tightened his hand around Goku's. He looked into Goku's eyes and said, "Goku, you must find the Dragon Balls. Before the eclipse. I'm sorry I cannot join you on this journey. Remember to always have faith in who you are."

Goku had a mission.

He must honor his grandfather's dying wish. First, he needed to talk to Master Roshi. Then, he'd find all seven Dragon Balls.

When the sun rose the next morning, Goku would go to Paozu.

CHAPTER FIVE

At dawn, Goku walked through what was left of his house. He couldn't figure out what had caused all the destruction.

In his grandpa's room, only one thing survived. It was an old iron chest. Goku very carefully lifted the lid.

Inside, neatly folded, was a pristine orange *gi*. The suit of a great master.

Goku took the gi out of the chest and gently touched the fabric. Holding the gi made him feel close to his grandfather.

"Some-
day I'll
beat
you."

GOKU

"I know it's here."

BULMA

"The first one to touch the ground loses."

GOKU VS. GOHAN

"Prepare to eat dirt!"

"True power comes from inside."

GOHAN

"DANGER IS MY MIDDLE NAME."

BULMA

"IT'S NOT HERE."

LORD PICCOLO

A noise outside distracted him. Gohan quickly put the gi back into the chest. Then he went to investigate.

Someone was walking through the house. From a hiding place, Goku watched the figure. He thought this might be the same person who ruined his home.

Goku prepared for a fight. He leapt into the room, but no one was there.

A second later, a bright red dot appeared on Goku's forehead. Goku knew that he could not fight against a laser gun.

"Where is it?" a girl demanded. "I know it's here." She shifted her gun slightly. The laser now pointed directly between Goku's eyes.

Goku wasn't afraid. "Are you Piccolo?"

he asked her.

"No." She didn't lower the gun. "My name's Bulma. Somebody stole my Promethium Orb. I'm here to get it back."

With her free hand, Bulma pulled out a handheld device. It was a radar grid. She activated the device. It beeped, blinking wildly.

"You have it!" she declared. Bulma tightened her fingers around her weapon.

Goku didn't want to get shot. In a swift move, he leapt out of her line of fire. Bulma fired anyway, but Goku dove away.

The gun blast missed him. But as he tumbled, the Dragon Ball flew out of his jacket.

The Dragon Ball thumped to the floor,

rolling halfway between Goku and Bulma. They both dove for it. Bulma got there first. She jumped back from Goku and pointed her gun at him again.

"Nice move," she told Goku. "But next time I shoot at you, I am not going to miss. My father found this Promethium Orb twenty years ago. You stole it from me and I'm not leaving without it."

Goku stared at Bulma. "I don't know what you're talking about. That's a Dragon Ball. Sushinchu, four-star ball. I promised my grandfather to keep it safe. No one is going to take it from me."

Bulma paused. "Did you say four stars?" She breathed deeply, shaking her head. "My Promethium Orb has five stars."

"Look at it," Goku told her.

Bulma checked out the Dragon Ball. Goku watched her counting the stars. "Oh my goodness!" she said. "I could have hurt you!" She dropped her gun.

"You weren't even close," Goku smiled. "What happened to your Dragon Ball?"

"A thief broke into my father's company, the Capsule Corporation." She told Goku everything. Someone wearing a jet pack had smashed the vault and taken her Dragon Ball.

"I swore to my father I'd get it back," Bulma said. "I followed the signal here. That's when I ran into you." She paused. "Sorry I shot at you. I thought you were the thief."

Goku laughed. "I'm lucky you aren't a better shot." Then he asked, "How did you know I have a Dragon Ball?"

"Look at this." Bulma showed Goku a small gadget with a high-tech screen. "This little machine can find Dragon Balls." When the machine was next to Goku's Dragon Ball, the screen went crazy. The radar grid flashed and beeped.

Goku was impressed. "You made a Dragon Ball energy locator."

"Dragon Ball Energy," Bulma repeated the phrase. "DBE. That's a catchy name. I've been calling it a Promethium Energy Extractor."

"PEE?" Goku chuckled. "Gross! DBE is a way better name."

Goku told Bulma about the seven Dragon Balls.

"I want to find them all," Bulma declared.

"Maybe we can help each other. I need to find Master Roshi in Paozu. Take me there, and I'll help you find the Dragon Balls," said Goku.

"I have a DBE. Why do I need you?" Bulma was used to working alone.

Goku pointed out the destroyed house. "Somebody else is looking for them," he told her. "You might need backup."

"Good point," Bulma agreed. It was decided.

Bulma and Goku would find the seven Dragon Balls together.

Outside the house, Bulma placed an oval-shaped capsule on the ground. She pushed a button on a remote control. With a flash, the capsule began to open. It unwrapped itself like a present. Then the small pieces inside grew and changed form. The metal parts clanged into place.

It only took a few minutes. But when it was done, the capsule had turned into a high-tech three-wheel speedster.

Bulma started the engine while Goku ran to the house to get a few things. When Goku came back, he had a backpack and his grandfather's bow staff.

"You know this is going to be risky," Goku warned Bulma.

"Danger is my middle name." Bulma told

him to climb on the bike seat behind her. They roared off.

In a distant jungle, Lord Piccolo came out of his airship. He walked over to the leader of a native village. The man wore a beautiful necklace. In the middle of the necklace hung the seven-starred Dragon Ball.

Lord Piccolo reached out and grabbed the Dragon Ball, ripping it from the man's neck. The tribal leader was so frightened, he let Lord Piccolo steal his prized possession.

Lord Piccolo held the Dragon Ball high, showing it off to Mai.

"I told you he would give it to me," Lord Piccolo announced.

Lord Piccolo and Mai boarded the airship.

THE DISCOVERY

They headed off to find the next Dragon Ball before Goku and Bulma!

The race was on.

ABOUT THE AUTHORS

Together Stacia Deutsch and Rhody Cohon have written more than twenty-one children's books in the past four years. In addition to their award-winning creative chapter book series entitled *Blast to the Past*, Stacia and Rhody have also ghostwritten for a popular girls' mystery series, published two nonfiction texts, and penned a young adult comedy. They have also written a number of junior movie tie-in novels for blockbuster films. Stacia lives in Irvine, California while Rhody lives in Tucson, Arizona.

Visit them at www.blasttothepastbooks.com.

GLOSSARY

KI – Your internal energy source, like a personal battery, that you access when you need more power.

SUSHINCHU – The Dragon Ball with four stars that Gohan gives his grandson, Goku, for his eighteenth birthday. There are seven Dragon Balls. To have your ultimate wish granted you must find all seven!

NAMEKS – An alien race that almost destroyed the earth two thousand years ago.

SHEN LONG – The Dragon that will grant a wish to the one who finds all seven Dragon Balls.

PAOZU – The hometown of Master Roshi, the ultimate trainer.

PROMETHIUM ORB – This is what Bulma initially calls the Dragon Ball. Hers has five stars.

COLLECT THEM ALL!

#1: THE DISCOVERY

DRAGONBALL EVOLUTION
Based on the movie from Twentieth Century Fox!

THE DISCOVERY
by Stacia Deutsch & Rhody Cohon
Screenplay by Ben Ramsey
Based upon the graphic novel series "Dragonball" by Akira Toriyama

#2: THE SEARCH

DRAGONBALL EVOLUTION
Based on the movie from Twentieth Century Fox!

THE SEARCH
by Stacia Deutsch & Rhody Cohon
Screenplay by Ben Ramsey
Based upon the graphic novel series "Dragonball" by Akira Toriyama

#3: THE BATTLE

DRAGONBALL EVOLUTION
Based on the movie from Twentieth Century Fox!

THE BATTLE
by Stacia Deutsch & Rhody Cohon
Screenplay by Ben Ramsey
Based upon the graphic novel series "Dragonball" by Akira Toriyama